Resisting Temptation
Overcoming and Surviving Addiction

Ursula Jones
Visionary Author

Co-Authored By:
Trimika Cooper, Claudia Massey,
Karen Robinson, Leona Smith,
Lisa Rodriguez Spaulding

Copyright © 2023 by Ursula Jones.
All Rights Reserved. This book, nor any portion thereof, may be reproduced or used in any manner whatsoever without the expressed written permission of the author(s) except for the use of brief quotations in a book review.

Printed in the United States of America.

ISBN: 979-8-9876649-6-4
Edited, Formatted and Published by Empower Her Publishing, LLC
empowerherpublishing.com

Table of Contents

Introduction..v

Friction Addiction........................……......1
Trimika Cooper

Temptation to Reclamation…....……......9
Ursula Jones

Therapeutic Addiction….....….…………25
Claudia Massey

Running Out Of – Running Into?……....35
Karen Robinson

Does Grief Ever End?………….……..…41
Leona Smith

Mi Vida Loca – My Crazy Life….……..…51
Lisa Rodriguez Spaulding

Conclusion……………………………....57

Introduction

The dictionary defines temptation as "the desire to do something, especially something wrong or unwise." Biblically, it is described as a situation in which one experiences a challenge between being loyal and disloyal to God's word. Temptation creeps up in various forms. Oftentimes, it's ever present when one is most vulnerable. These instances of vulnerability often include times of grief, sadness, or discomfort. Circumstances have usually brought an individual to a lonely place and they're seeking refuge in substances, people, or behaviors that are not good for them.

In this book, *Resisting Temptation, Overcoming and Surviving Addiction*, six dynamic women share their personal stories of battling times in their lives that forced them into temptation. They each bring unique and diverse experiences surrounding the topic of the disease that is addiction. Recognizing that old habits die hard, they each fight to overcome the negative thoughts and emotions that encompass their hearts and minds and fight ferociously to get back to living a healthy, addiction-free lifestyle.

At the end of the day, each author acknowledges God as their Savior, and attests that without Him, they would not have been able to overcome the challenges surrounding temptation that once held them down. If you are undergoing a struggle with temptation, or having a hard time overcoming addiction, it is our hope that after reading this book, you find refuge, strength, encouragement and hope to overcome and survive addiction too.

Friction Addiction
Trimika Cooper

"What are you doing after your next client?" Gina asked.

"I'm not sure. I don't have another client until 5, so I will probably go home, cook, and take a nap," I responded. But little did Gina know, I was going home to pleasure my sugar basin. I didn't have time this morning because I woke up late and right about now, my body is going through withdrawals.

Having a high sex drive can be challenging. Wanting and needing pleasure all the time and sometimes at the wrong time. I have always been strong in my faith and as a babe in Christ, I would wonder if self-gratification was a sin. I know we were created to please God and not ourselves. Pleasing myself should not be my driving force, but right now it is. "Oh Lord, please take these urges away from me," I prayed. And as I prayed, I would feel my sugar basin throb.

Trimika Cooper

After being molested as a child, my first encounter with sex was with a female. She would try to finger me but didn't know where the opening was; therefore, she would push her finger on my vulva and it would hurt so bad to the point where I have never allowed anyone to put their finger on my sugar basin. Growing up as a teenager, my friends would talk about getting fingered but I didn't see how it felt good. I guess I'm just scarred from a bad experience. My abuser would give me oral sex daily and after a while, I started to need it. Now as an adult, I can't get enough of vaginal stimulation.

In my early 20's, I was offered a part-time job selling sex toys. I thought, sure, I'll take that job. As a hairstylist I had a lot of clients who I knew for sure would have parties so I could definitely make a profit. I began having parties every Friday and Saturday nights, and even some Sunday evenings too. Business was going great, up until I had a party one night and this lady asked me questions about my product that I couldn't answer. She then said, "how can you sell something and you don't know how it works?" She was right - how could I? So after that night, I went home and did research on the origin of sex toys. I found out that it started around 29,000 BC when what is now called Germany began carving rocks into phallic shapes. It's not known for sure if they were used for sex toys, fertility ceremonies, or if they just carved penis rocks for fun. Either way, they paved the way for the sex toy industry. In 500 BC, things got a little more innovative when the ancient Greeks started making fake dongs using different kinds of materials. Some were made out of brass or stuffed leather and they were called olisbokollikes, which is not an easy word to pronounce. The Greeks also started making lube by using olives to make olive oil. I began to read more and more and was very intrigued. The ancient time people were freaky. I found out the word dildo came into play around 1400 AD during the Italian renaissance. It stems from diletto, which means pleasure. By the time I finished doing my research, I was a sex toy scholar. The only thing left to do was to try some of the products I was selling. I decided to start with the product the lady had asked about at the party. It was called a Bullet. That bullet changed my life and my whole trajectory as to how I looked at my product. It gave me the most powerful, explosive orgasms I have ever had, which happened so quickly. It made my toes curl and my whole body convulse and lock in a position I thought would be permanent. The steam that radiated from my body was like Arizona rays - dry, smoldering heat. The high pitched scream that came from my mouth was like a high octave Opera singer. As you may know, the clitoris typically has two DNCs, which means "dorsal nerve of the clitoris". These are the nerves that transmit sensations that ultimately end up in your brain. My sensations were telling my brain "I LIKE THIS FEELING!"

After introducing myself to the bullet, I was hooked. I started buying all sorts of toys. I was my best customer, using the toys every chance I got. Who needed a man when I had BOB, my "battery operated boyfriend" in different shapes and sizes. I was so wrapped up in my toys that if I didn't have a party, I was home playing with them. On every lunch break, I went home to feel the friction on my sugar basin. It was like I needed that quick jolt run through my body. It was the best stress and pain reliever I ever had. In the 1800's-era, English men began labeling anxious or unhappy women with Hysteria. Aiming to have those women relax, they were treated with intense genital stimulation. They say Hysteria began to spread like wildfire, and the doctors couldn't keep up, so they began to make vibrating machines to make women orgasm with less effort. I can definitely see why; this was a convenient, feel-good tool.

I used my vibrators so much that my body ached from being contorted and stuck in different positions. My stomach, especially. The muscles felt like I had worked out three times a day, but there was no way I could let this feeling go. My vibrators replaced me receiving oral sex. The vibrations made everything going on in my mind stop. I can remember one night I was using my vibrator and it felt so good. I used it for a while and it drained me. The orgasms were so strong, making my body shake and distort until my stomach muscles hurt. But the feeling was so unreal that I continued using BOB. I woke up the next morning and tried to get out of bed but I was paralyzed from the waist down. My legs were so heavy I couldn't lift them up. I began to cry and I called my momma. She came right over. I was so scared and didn't know what was going on. My mom asked, "what did you do?" Hesitant to respond, "Nothing," I said. "I used my vibrator off and on all night and that's it." My mother had worked in the medical field and had seen some crazy things in the ER. She was able to get me to Urgent Care and I was so embarrassed, but I was more afraid of what was going on with my body. The doctor said that I used the vibrator too long and the stimulation was too much for the nerves causing me to lose the sensation in my legs. The good thing is that it was just temporary, but very scary for me.

After that, I knew I had to stop. Thinking I was paralyzed made me realize that I was over using my toys. I'm not saying that I stopped using my toys automatically, but I did slow down and didn't use them as long. It was a slow process and it didn't happen overnight. I now know that self-gratification is not my driving force, but pleasing God is. Ultimate pleasure comes as a result of crucifying our flesh and abandoning ourselves to the higher purpose of God (Luke 9:23). I am now happily married and understand that Proverbs 5:18-19 tells us to rejoice in our spouse and be captivated by their love. Know that sexuality was intended not only for us to procreate, but for pleasure and enjoyment with our spouse. It's definitely an important way to build intimacy together.

Addictions may not all be the same, but they can change the dynamics of one's ability to make good decisions. Some addictions break up households or even hurt loved ones. Anyone with an addiction needs love and support, not judgement, from others. My addiction was something I kept from people because I thought I was the only one with this problem, but I wasn't. It was like my dirty little secret. No I didn't need rehab for my addiction, but some addicts do. My addiction may sound strange to some people, but it's a real one. Sex toys are a billion-dollar industry now and still on the rise. I know couples who have been married 15 or more years that use sex toys to spice it up in the bedroom. In my opinion, what goes on in a married couple's bedroom is their business as long as they aren't allowing the toys to come between their intimacy and bond.

I hope my story brings insight to other addictions. People aren't always addicted to drugs, but my addiction was like a drug to me. I needed it multiple times a day. Was it because I didn't have a man? I don't know. But whatever the reason, it hooked me really fast. I'm glad I have been set free from my friction addiction and I hope my story is helpful to others.

Trimika Cooper is from Chadbourn, NC, but is a resident of Charlotte, NC where she lives with her husband, Genatus Cooper. She is the mother of four children: Sharmane, Destinee,

Marcus, and Jayden, grandmother to three granddaughters: Amina, Angel, and Anissa and also has a fur baby named Grace. She is an ordained minister who loves helping those in need. Trimika is also an Assistant Director at Harris Learning Academy, CEO of Cooper's Creative Stylez Balloon Décor, Faith Family & Fabulous Hair T-shirt line, Visionary Author of Amazon's #1 Best-Selling book, *4Ms: Muted Molestation that Manifested Mentally*, Co-Author of Amazon's #1 Best-Selling book, *Reclaiming My Life*, which has a Podcast on Youtube, and Co-Author of the forthcoming *The Final Chapter: Reclaiming My Life After the Storm*.

Keep in touch with Trimika:
Facebook: Min Trimika Cooper
Facebook: Cooper's Creative Stylez
Instagram: Coopers_ Creative_ Stylez

Acknowledgements

Marcus Solomon
No More Closed Doors The Podcast on YouTube; Co-Author in 4M's
Website: Marcus-Solomon.com;
https://youtube.com/@Marcus..Solomon?si=_Ubp-kjZVu48PDkf
Facebook: @Marcus Devone Solomon
Instagram: @d.evoneee
LinkedIn: https://www.linkedin.com/in/marcus-solomon-888a05236

Genatus Cooper
D.O.C. Definition of Cool LLC Clothing Brand and DJ Bucho
Facebook: Genatus Cooper

Destinee' Solomon
Scentsy by Dee
desolomon.scentsy.us
Facebook: Destinee' Solomon
Instagram: @Desiw.abook

Temptation to Reclamation
Ursula Jones

Back Story…

Let me tell my story of how I messed my life completely up and got it right back, how I took a mess and turned it into a message. Years ago, I had a drug addiction. I will never forget it. It was right after I had my last child. I think my baby was about a year old at the time. His dad left me right before I had the baby to go back to his girlfriend. I became really depressed because I had already had three children with three different fathers. And I struggled with them. So when I got with my last baby's father, I just knew we were going to be together forever. But somehow it didn't happen like that. His dad was so independent. He made sure I had everything I needed. He was a man. A jealous man. But a real man. We were young and foolish and he didn't really know what he wanted at that time.

Ursula Jones

Well the day I went into labor, Ray decided he wanted to go back with his ex and he did. He came to the hospital briefly but his mom was there with me the whole entire time. He stayed just long enough to see the baby and then left me to go back to his ex. In hindsight, she was probably still his girlfriend, not his ex like he told me, because she took him back after finding out that I was pregnant by him. He claimed after seeing the baby that he may not be his baby because the baby was really light, about white, and the word on the streets was that I had messed around with a white man. Now of course I knew it was Ray's baby. So I wanted to hurt him for saying that. We had been seeing each other for over a year and for him to do that to me was unbelievable. I thought back to myself, is this how people do? Are you like the other men I've dated? Heartless? I couldn't believe how Ray had changed overnight. He left the hospital and told me he couldn't sign the birth certificate because he may not be the father. This hurt me to the core. I knew I had slept with several men but when I got with Ray, I was faithful. Just the heck of him. Nevertheless, I named my baby after Ray, Ray Devone Jones Jr., because I knew that was his dad. I called him Lil' Ray. He looked just like Ray when he came out of me, but just highlighted. You know when babies are born they are lighter; well some, but after a few days they get their color. Within the next week or two he was dark brown. He was Ray's twin. He slept just like his dad as a baby too. I couldn't even believe it.

Temptation to Reclamation

One day Ray came to see the baby and me and said he wanted to take the baby and raise him himself. I had already had three children I was struggling with. I did not want to struggle with Lil' Ray too so I let him take the baby and raise him. I cried for days, couldn't eat, couldn't sleep. Every time a car came down the dirt road I stayed on, I would peek out the window hoping and praying it was him. Hoping and praying he would stop being foolish and just settle down with me and be one happy family. But he didn't. He lived in Jacksonville, N.C. with his girlfriend. And the only reason why I knew the address is because she made him take out child support on me and the address was on the paperwork. When I received the papers I couldn't believe what I saw. I couldn't believe him. How do you stay with me for over a year and do this? What kind of man does this to a woman who really loves you? A dog! I was broken, torn up inside that I ever had a child with him. Later, I received blood test results that I never requested that stated Lil' Ray was 99.99% Ray's child. I called social services right away and asked how they could do a blood test without me even being there. They told me they can use the stuff they already had and only needed the baby and his medical card. I was happy Ray found out he really was his baby but mad how dirty he was to do a paternity test. You dirty dog! Do you even have a heart or are you so dumb in love with your girl that you'd do whatever she wants you to do. Honey, I gave you a whole baby that took you over 30 years to get. You couldn't even have a baby by the other women and you thought something was wrong with you. Now look at God! I have a baby with you and you act like this. Fine!

As time went by, I began to slowly get over him. I didn't keep my baby until he was more than six months old and he was so spoiled 'til it didn't make sense. Ray and I would take turns keeping him but he had custody of him. Once he got about a year old, I was over Ray. I started dating other guys just to take my mind off of him. My best friend Melissa knew my whole situation. I began to hang out at her house a lot because she kept a lot of company and it kept my mind off of Ray. I had a little freedom because my children were old enough to do things by themselves, so I would walk across the dirt road and go over to Melissa's house. One day I went over to her house and her long-time ex-boyfriend, Rob, was over there. Even though they weren't together for such a long time, he still came by to see her every now and then. Anyway, one day as I was walking home from Melissa's house, he drove past my house. I lived in a mobile home park that had a bad dirt road. When you came down the road, you had to drive slowly because it was so bad. I had my own home in that park and was renting to buy my own land. My home was in my dad's name because at the time of purchase, I had no credit and my dad (bless the dead) wanted only the best for me so he put it in his name after talking it over with his wife so I could have my own. My dad didn't want me to waste my money on rent another year.

Anyway, as I was going home, he was riding by and stopped. I let him in. He never knew of me, only Ray because they worked together at a hog farm together years ago, before I even knew Ray. I was so vulnerable at this time. I was lonely and I wanted to be loved. Remember, I told you I was also foolish. So he came in and asked if he could take me to Dallas Seafood. During that time, that seafood place was in Clarkton, N.C. and was the best seafood in that town. I told him even though I wasn't best friends with Melissa when they dated, and it had been years ago, I still didn't want to talk to her ex. So he left. Well he came back at another time after leaving Melissa's house and that time I gave in. Again, I was foolish, and was desperate for what he had in his pants. I wanted some sex. I wanted whatever at the moment and he was a cutie, a woman's lover, and he had game for real. I knew he was a dog, but at that time I didn't care. He wasn't anything like Ray. Ray cared about my feelings, my kids, my financial state, my needs. He was very independent. He just wanted multiple women and that wasn't happening with me. This guy was a drug dealer. He wanted me just to sell drugs at my house, which was another spot to get the cops off him at his home. He only wanted to take me out to eat, go to the movies, hang out, and to screw. He was a dog and lied about the women he saw under cover. He said they were on drugs but they really weren't. He was sleeping with them all. But at that time, I couldn't see anything. I just wanted to have fun.

Now of course, my friend lives across from me and she began to see her ex's car over my house several times. She knew me and she knew what I'd do behind closed doors. She figured out what was going on and was heated. She sent her baby girl to my house with a five-page letter. I will never forget when I saw her walking to my house. She knocked on my screen door and came in and said, "my momma told me to give this to you." I stood in the middle of my floor wondering what in the world she had written in this letter. It must be bad if she sent her baby girl to give it to me. I opened up the letter. I still have it to this day and it's been over 20 years. A couple things that hit my soul hard is when she wrote I was the biggest whore of N.C. and that I could win a reward for sleeping with so many men. She was my best friend. She knew everything about me - who I slept with, when, where, what time, everything. After reading it, I was upset because I could feel her hurt and pain in that letter she wrote. She was my only friend. And a real friend. During this time, friends were hard to come by, so I loved her like a sister. Me being stupid, foolish, and dumb, I chose what was in that man's pants over our friendship.

At this time in my life, I didn't drink alcohol, smoke cigarettes or use any drugs. But once I got with this guy, the drug dealer, I started

Temptation to Reclamation

smoking cigarettes, would pull a blunt every now and then, but no hard drugs or alcohol. They say you are the company you keep and that's a true statement. Melissa left me alone completely. I was so foolish and down for Rob, I didn't even care. I had been hurt by men so I became heartless. I just wanted what I wanted and that was it. One day another friend of mine was at the store in Clarkton called Jones. It was right beside the grocery store. I remember being at the cash register and Rob called hollering, "where are you?" I told him, "I'm at Jones getting a few things before I come home." He said just like this, "come straight home." I said, "ok." Now, I became scared of Rob because what I didn't know is that he was a woman beater and that he was soooo jealous. One day months before this, I was chilling in my van with a neighbor and he was smoking weed. Well I noticed Rob coming down the dirt road and me not thinking he would get mad, didn't move. We sat right there while he pulled up. He got out of his car and pulled a gun on my neighbor, who was a male, and pointed it at him until he was out of sight. He then made me get in his car. He drove to Rico, not far from where we lived, where a bad curve was and made me get out of the car. Before I knew it, he had put the gun to my head and made me promise to never do that again and to never cheat on him. I was scared out of my mind. I was like what in the world have I gotten myself into. He actually said he would kill me. After that, I was so scared of him I never did anything like that again. And I never told a soul.

Ursula Jones

So after he told me to come straight home, me being so scared of him, I did just that. I got home and Ann, an older friend who grew up with me in the community and was living with me because she dated his brother, said, "Rob is mad with you." I began to be scared all over again. I called his cell phone but he never answered. I repeatedly called him back to back for about three hours or so, no answer. So now I was mad because he wasn't answering after he requested for me to come straight home. Later that night we got a phone call that he got shot about eight times and was dead. Whoever we talked to that night (I can't remember) said go to Red Hill Road. Ann drove because I was so messed up after hearing this. I couldn't believe it. I cried all the way there. At that time in my life I hadn't lost anyone I was so close to. This was a feeling I wouldn't want anyone to feel. We were only together for about eight months and I loved him, even though I was scared of him. Once we got there, they had yellow tape everywhere. He got shot at his baby mama's house. They said her boyfriend killed him. I was too scared to even get to the bottom of it. Besides, it wasn't like we had been together for years and I didn't have any kids with him.

That night was one of the worst nights of my life. When we got back home, my friends tried to keep me calm as much as possible. I was so scared to take a bath, use the bathroom, drive alone, really anything, because in the little time we did spend together, we became close. So

Ann waited on me hand and foot. I begged her to stay there with me for awhile until I was able to get myself back together and she did. I didn't have to move a muscle. Once Melissa found out Rob got killed, she walked to my house and hugged me so tight. I cried so bad on her shoulders because after all I had done to her, I still loved her and she still loved me. I apologized for what I did to her and she forgave me, but I was still hurt about Rob. She gave me money for food and to get me something for the funeral. She was still my friend and I was blessed to have her as one. This taught me a valuable lesson: to never bite the hand that feeds you.

After everything was over, I was depressed. The crowd I kept at my house did drugs. By this time, I only smoked weed since getting with Rob and cigarettes. Well they introduced me to cocaine. I had always said I would never do cocaine. And especially not put it up my nose. I thought that was insane to do such a thing, but I did it. Once I did, I said, "It's not doing anything. What is it supposed to do?" They said, "Keep doing it. You will feel it, and once you feel it, you will know." So I did. I kept doing it.

And before I knew it, I was…**Addicted!**

I loved how it made me feel. I had no worries at this time. I was getting so high I was forgetting about Rob. Once I got hooked all I did was snort powder (as they called it) all day. I began to smoke more cigarettes and even drink alcohol. After I got introduced to cocaine, I began to hate marijuana. It was a slow high and I didn't want it. Cocaine kept me busy, my mind busy, me hyped up and I liked that at that time. Sadly though, I couldn't afford the cocaine. I was introduced to the loan shops around the way and borrowed money until I was in such a terrible, deep debt I couldn't even see my way out of. My best friend begged me to stop and get help but I was so addicted. I couldn't and didn't want the help. I became really bad with this addiction. When we would go out to party, I would sit in my van and just snort cocaine. I started doing it so much I didn't even want to go out anymore. All I wanted to do was stay in my room and snort cocaine with my friends with my room door locked. This was a weekend thing. It was my new hobby. My friends always counted on me to get the cocaine on credit because they knew I could get loans from the loan shops. If I didn't get the money from the loan shops, I would sleep with men for it. Whoever! Please don't point a finger or shake your head. I had an addiction. It was bad. Cocaine will make you do stuff you would never do. Lie, steal, cheat, have sex for it and any and everything else.

Titus 2:12: "It teaches us to say 'NO' to ungodliness and worldly passions, and to live self-controlled, upright and godly lives in this present age." This verse means the grace of God teaches you to resist worldly passions and anything which is not godly, including alcohol addiction and drug addiction. I completely ruined my character behind my drug addiction. You see, I lost a loved one and went into depression. At the time, it looked and felt like I had no way out. I became addicted to cocaine, borrowed money I didn't have, had sex with multiple people to keep my habit going, and then entered a dark place. I felt hopeless, so I kept doing it. I got down to the lowest part of my life. I began to call on God. My lights were off for over two weeks and my children witnessed this. I prayed and prayed for God to help me get out of this mess. I prayed from my heart and I even told God, I said "God, I will stop this mess. Please help me." I began to tell Him, "if I do it again, take the life out of me." That prayer I prayed scared me so bad, I was too scared to ever do it again. That prayer was sincerely from my heart. Months went by and I was still in terrible debt because I owed the loan shops and I was terribly afraid of them. If you owed them money, they could kill you or would do something bad to you at minimum. I kept praying because I knew what I promised God and I didn't want to go back on my word. So I trusted Him and believed that I would get through this, even when it didn't look like I would.

One day I went to meet Ray to get my son. That day was different because he came to me and said, "I want to make things right." I was shocked, but I listened to him before I said anything. He said, "I want to get back with you. And do it right." At that time I was sleeping around with a guy named Mike. I was told he was kin to me down the line. But anyway, he was only there for a hot meal, a warm, clean house, and my private. He was only good for under the sheets. I knew if I gave Ray another chance and let him know what I expected from him and what I would allow and not allow, he would do good. The only real problem I had with him was he couldn't keep his thing in his pants. At this point, I had nothing to lose, so I gave him another try and it's the best move I ever made. I had a long talk with him and he listened to me. I told him about what all I did after Rob got killed and he understood. When he got his income tax money, he said, "Tell me all who you owe. I don't want this to interfere with our life." He went and paid my over six-thousand dollar debt off and just like that, I was debt-free. Won't God do it?!!! I promised I wouldn't do cocaine again and I didn't. Now I didn't stop smoking cigarettes until August 2012. But my God, I'm so thankful.

Ray and I married years after that on May 4, 2009. We became a family. My life wasn't perfect, but it was near to it. We had a few kick-backs, but nothing that was not fixable. Look at how God showed up and showed out. I've been clean for over 19 years and happily married. We later moved to Texas where my husband continued his construction career. I own and operate a small cleaning business called Rj Cleaning Services LLC, named after Ray and Lil' Ray. I'm also a notary for the state of Texas. I work 48 hours a week at a warehouse. I'm a whole different person. See, when I didn't see no way out, God had already had a plan for me. The mess I went through turned into a message. To you out there who has a drug addiction, and feels like there's no hope, there's no way to stop, believe there is. Seek God. Get help. Never give up. You can do all things through Christ who strengthens you.

My message to my family and friends: God has forgiven me. I know I may have shamed my loved ones, but I'm not where I used to be. I ask that you please don't judge me from my past. Look at me now. I'm healed and free. I have a testimony so I had to share my own story. This is my truth. I have Reclaimed My Life. Temptation To Reclamation.

Ursula Jones is a native of Council, NC and currently resides in Lake Jackson, Texas. She is married to Ray Jones, is a mother of four beautiful children - Kareem, Cedina, Fatima, and Ray Jr., and grandmother to six - Trinity, Jakari, Jakeem, Journey, KJ, and Mason. Ursula is the Founder and Owner of Rj Cleaning Services LLC and a Notary/ Loan Signing Agent in the state of TX. She works a full-time job as a warehouse/forklift operator and is also a digital creator on Facebook. Ursula is a member of House of

Prayer and Praise Ministries and helps feed the homeless. She is a co-author of four best-selling collaboration books on Amazon: *Reclaiming My Life*, *I'm Not Your Superwoman*, *After the Storm* and *4Ms: Muted Molestation that Manifested Mentally*. Ursula loves spending time with family, traveling, shopping, and living life to the fullest. God is the head of her life and through Him, all things are possible. She trusts His plan for her life and allows Him to guide her footsteps to GREATER.

Connect with Ursula on the web:

Facebook: Ursula Jones
Instagram: @prissyjvlogs
YouTube: Prissyj Vlogs
Website: linktr.ee/prissyjvlogs

Acknowledgements

Patricia Finney
Trinity Creations
Facebook: Patricia Finney
Instagram: @Pfinney0316
LinkedIn: Patricia Finney

Lisa Spaulding
L&C Personal Touch
Facebook: @lisarodriguezspaulding
LinkedIn: Lisa Spaulding

Therapeutic Addiction
Claudia Massey

Exhausted, I'm awakened by my cell phone ringing on the hotel nightstand. I jump up in bed hysterically and glance over at the clock. It's 3:04 am. The unfamiliar number is an indication it's the hospital regarding my mother and nothing can prepare me for the words waiting at the swipe of the Answer button.

"Hello," I answer. "Mrs. Massey?" the nurse confirms. "Yes," I respond. "I'm terribly sorry but your mother has passed away. You're welcome to come and see her if you'd like." Honestly, I didn't hear any words beyond "mother," but assumed she extended that much to me. Life as I had always known it up until that point had come to an end.

Completely numb, I put down the phone and sobbed like a baby. My husband was comforting, but nothing could take this pain away. I don't have a Mama anymore! Finally, I calm my tears enough to call my brother then go to the room next door to tell my children. Imaginably, they are devastated.

We all get dressed and head to New Hanover Regional Medical Center in Wilmington, NC where my mother had been on a ventilator for the past week. The doctors had been telling us that her options were slim to none. Prior to today, August 2, 2015, she had suffered two strokes and a heart attack within a month and a half's time. I remember my brother calling me early in the summer to tell me that something wasn't right with our mother. "She woke up from a nap mumbling and slurring her words," he had said. I told him it sounded like symptoms of a stroke. When I called my mom, she sounded like herself. I still urged her to visit the hospital, but she refused. My family and I drove to North Carolina from Richmond, Virginia as planned. My mother had recently retired from a 25-year career as a caregiver and was moving to Virginia to live with me that weekend. She had worked tirelessly for so long and I was glad that she finally accepted my invitation to come rest and enjoy life.

The weekend was perfect as were all weekends that I was able to return home and spend time with my mom. After indulging in her infamous cooking, attending church on Sabbath as Seventh-day Adventists and staying up all night chit-chatting, Sunday morning woke us all in a frenzy when my daughter rushed to the front room yelling, "Something's wrong with Grandma!" We all leaped to our feet and ran to my mother's room to discover she was having a seizure. "Call 911!" I shouted. It took EMS nearly an hour to arrive. This was a disadvantage I did not appreciate about growing up in the country.

On the twenty-minute ride to the hospital, my mother suffered her first real stroke and by the time we reached the hospital, she was unconscious and her left side was drooped. She spent the next few weeks in the hospital recovering, undergoing several tests, minor exercises, diet changes, medications and recovery plans. Ultimately, my weekend visit turned into a one-month hospital stay during her transition before rehab. There was no way I was leaving my mother's side when she needed me the most.

Once she was discharged and placed at a rehab facility, I left for a day to come home and celebrate my birthday with my family and for years, I've fought myself over that decision because I feel like it led me to this moment. My mother had a second stroke and a heart attack in rehab. When I told her I'd see her later, I never imagined it would be this way. For a full week, my brother and I were faced with the hardest decision of our lives regarding our mother's quality of life if she survived.

Claudia Massey

When we finally arrived at the hospital and I laid eyes on my mother, it was too difficult to accept that she was gone. I needed my mother. She was my best friend – the one I spoke to every day, multiple times a day. I relied on her for so much. How was life supposed to go on? How would I survive without her?

After laying my mother to rest on August 9, 2015, I didn't know what to do with myself. Shortly after, my husband was deployed, so not only was I grieving, but I felt like I had to grieve alone. Initially, I grieved like most people grieve, I believe. I spent my days in the bed shedding countless tears, reflecting on the series of events that led to my mom's passing, including all the "what if's". I'm a mom of six - three biological children and three adopted children. Although I desperately wanted not to give a care in the world, I knew that at some point, I would have to pick up the pieces and really resume my motherly duties. My children still needed me. But how? It was hard to function through the pain. I couldn't stop thinking about my mom, wanting her, needing her to come back to me. I needed something to help take my mind off my incredible loss.

Initially, I just wanted to get out of the house. I knew that if I stepped out of the house, it would be easier to also step out of my sad thoughts. My oldest daughter and I had just started a business, Patience for Patients Homecare, which honored my mom's legacy, so I felt like if we got out and did some networking, that would keep my mind busy. It worked for a while, but it wasn't enough. Pretty soon, I started saying, "let's run by the store" after our meetings. "Running to the store" then became routine. I wanted to go to the store for something and nothing at all. I just needed to buy something to make me feel better. Shopping allowed me to both get out of the house and focus on something "new" in my life. This is when I fully understood the phrase "retail therapy".

Eventually, though, local shopping just wasn't enough. I needed to feed my craving to spend money on a higher level. I wanted to go bigger, get away. This led to me wanting to travel. At first, it was local trips, like Richmond to Williamsburg, VA to shop at the outlets and grab some lunch during the day. Then it progressed to weekend getaways still within driving distance. Soon enough, I needed to book a flight. I needed a real escape - from my home, my life, and the reality that my mom was no longer here. So traveling became my new addiction. I would take a trip somewhere, come home, and be ready to book my next flight. I realized that having idle time at home took me to a sad place and I didn't want to be there, so I left every chance I could. I needed to be gone - even now - eight years later.

During my time spent at home, I didn't feel like doing much of anything. Cooking was one of those things. Again, my husband was deployed so I didn't have the responsibilities of a wife and two of my children were adults at this point. Kabuto's Japanese Steakhouse is my favorite restaurant. Because I didn't have the energy to do much around the house, I realized that I began going to eat at Kabuto's a lot more frequently. I was an emotional eater and Kabuto's was my comfort food. Most times, I would invite all my girls (my children) for us to all be together. I needed and wanted to be surrounded by them as much as possible. Before I knew it, I was there at least four to five times a week, spending nearly $3,000 a month in dining out at that restaurant alone.

As time passed, I realized that I had developed some bad habits as coping mechanisms. While being addicted to spending money on particular things to deflect my grief wasn't causing physical harm to me or others, in some instances, I was not being a good steward of my funds. I recognized that there were better ways for me to heal and that required self-reflection and adjustments. During my time of reflection, I began thinking of ways that I could turn my grieving into greatness. More specifically, I wanted to ensure that my mother's legacy lived on while simultaneously giving me a reason to celebrate versus grieve. This is when I founded Rena's New Life Ministry, a community-based organization that gives back to those in need. My mother gave to those in need my entire life, even when she didn't have it to give. I could hear her saying, "Claudia, if you're gonna spend money, put it towards something good instead of things you don't need." So that's what I did.

Rena's New Life Ministry provides financial assistance to displaced families, creates an annual Christmas Miracle Shopping Experience for struggling moms, hosts an annual Back-to-School book bag drive, offers a monthly college incentive stipend to one deserving student per year, provides an annual scholarship towards Christian education for one student per year, plus so much more. This ministry not only gives "new life" to those who benefit from its support, but also gives me a reason to overturn my negative emotions surrounding my mom's passing, use my money for the greater good and also feel good about continuing my mom's legacy while helping others just like she did.

Moreover, when it came to traveling, I decided to view my need to get away from a different lens. Yes, I did and do want to escape, but it doesn't have to be as a distraction from my grief. I've been a mom since I was 19 years old and now at 52, I have six children. Of course, four of them are adults, but three of my daughters who I adopted 12 years ago are special needs. So even at 25, 19 and 17 years old, they still require a great deal of attention, patience and care. I'm also a wife, a grandmother to two, a business owner, among a host of other roles. I absolutely deserve to book a flight and let my hair down from time to time. Traveling is no longer just a distraction; it's a form of self-care for me to go, recharge and come back home refreshed to be all the things I'm required to be.

Now, I do still love my Kabuto's food, but I have limited myself to only going one to two times a week versus four to five. Of course, I'm still grieving, but I'm a lot better now and have fully resumed my motherly and wifely duties, which include cooking!

Grief can easily lead to depression which clouds your mind and judgement. We don't think sensibly. We make careless decisions and sometimes, even when we're better, after doing it for so many years, these decisions become habitual. I do think about all of the money I could've saved, but I don't regret what I did when I did it because at that time, it was the comfort I needed. Now, particularly as a Life and Wellness Coach, I recognize that addiction looks differently for everyone. Essentially, it's just unhealthy habits. In order to overcome those unhealthy habits, you must be open to self-reflection and be willing to make the changes necessary to live a more fulfilling life. I'm still grieving the loss of my mom, but thank God I've been delivered from indulging in behavior that only masks my pain. If you too are living with distractions that you know are not good, I encourage you to get the help you need to overcome. This may look like a self-healing journey like mine. It may look like professional counseling. It may just require you talking with someone you trust. Whatever you need to get past your addictions, do that. You deserve to live a life that is free of mental, emotional, financial and physical bondage.

Claudia R. Massey is a resident of Richmond, Virginia where she devotes much of her time being a wife to her husband, James, and together, they have eight children, three of whom they adopted out of foster care. She is the Co-Founder of **Patience for Patients, LLC**, a non-medical homecare agency that provides personal care and companionship services to the geriatric population. Claudia attends Courthouse Road Church of Seventh-Day Adventists where she is a devoted member and Women's Ministry Leader. She is a Radio Host at Radio Poder 1380 AM, a TV Host at Preach

Claudia Massey

The Word Worldwide Network, a Certified Life and Wellness Coach, The Visionary Author of Amazon's #1 Best-Sellers, *Reclaiming My Life* and *After the Storm*, co-author of Amazon's #1 Best-Seller, *4Ms: Muted Molestation that Manifested Mentally*, and a Columnist for Diva Dynasty Magazine. Claudia's most recent achievement is being an Honoree for The President Biden Volunteer Award! In her very spare time, she enjoys traveling with her family, feeding the homeless at local shelters and giving back to those in need through a family initiative she founded in memory of her mom, **Rena's New Life Ministry**. To those who know Claudia, she is known as one of the sweetest and strongest people one will ever meet. Her compassion for people, even during her own adversities and trials is truly unmatched.

Keep in touch with Claudia:

Website: contactclaudiamassey.com
Facebook: @coachclaudiamassey
Instagram: @coachclaudiamassey

Running Out Of - Running Into?
Karen Robinson

I can do all things through Christ who strengthens me. Philippians 4:13

When you hear the word "addiction," drugs tend to be the initial association. The truth of the matter is, you can be addicted to anything. The Oxford American Writer's Thesaurus defines addiction as: dependency, dependence, craving, habit, weakness, compulsion, fixation, enslavement.

I had a habit, a habit of running! Every time I got into a relationship, the first sign of trouble, I was out the door. It all started way back before I can remember. My first example of running, however, was when my father ran and left my mother and me when I was a child. It left me feeling empty and with no knowledge of what it was like to receive a father's love and care. The fact that I was always running from my problems led me to a bigger problem: lots of unfinished business and love-hate relationships dangling. Ironically enough, my co-addiction was getting married. I loved the idea of being asked to be someone's wife, but I lacked the ability to stick it out and build. My first marriage, however, did not deserve me staying and sticking it out because it was turbulent and filled with violence. There was no reason for me to stay so I ran as far away as possible hiding from my abusive husband. Afraid and still very young, I spent four years in that marriage before finally gaining the courage to leave. One child was produced in that marriage, a beautiful baby girl. I didn't have to worry about him seeing my daughter because as soon as he remarried, his wife made sure she stood between my daughter and her father, preventing them from having a relationship.

Seven years later, I remarried. I thought for sure this was it. Muscular, chocolate, and a professional man. I'd never dated a chocolate man before; they just weren't my preference. However, this one caught my eye. He showed a strong interest in me and I fell for it, bait and hook. I was always told no man wants a woman with children, but he accepted my children so that was enough for me. What I didn't know was he was quite the ladies' man. Always helpful and friendly! Too friendly, over friendly. There was a shortage of gentlemen, but he knew how to lay it on thick. Carrying groceries, doing laundry, opening car doors, holding your umbrella while you walk in the rain, looking deep into your soul with those brown eyes. Yep, he was quite the gentleman! He asked me to be his wife and I accepted. Down the aisle I went. We had a beautiful wedding! I felt complete, yet empty. I didn't take the time to learn what being his wife entailed. Not to mention, I wasn't nearly as

Running Out Of – Running Into?

spiritual as I needed to be to fight what was coming down the pipe for me. There were so many errors made on both of our behalves that led to our marriage ending bitterly by divorce. Instead of talking things through and coming to a healthy resolve, my addiction was in full force and in control of me. I laced up my sneakers and began to run.

One year later, I'm going down the aisle again. Well, not down the aisle because this time it was a low-budget ceremony right at the courthouse in front of a magistrate. My new groom and I agreed to love each other through sickness and health, for richer or poorer, until death do us part. We were definitely poor. Couldn't get the ends to meet. We were young and what I thought was in love. We were a blended family and had a systematic way of living. This I thought was really it because it was lasting. We reached year 11 and I was honestly happy…until my then husband began to have an affair with a co-worker. I didn't know how to handle that. Of course, my first thought was to run. My running shoes were a little rusty because this was what I considered a long-term marriage. However, after many failed attempts to restore the marriage, I gave in to my addiction and ran. I filed for divorce and we went our separate ways. Here I was again, left broken and to pick up the pieces.

Not long after that came the rebound man. I just didn't realize that's who he was to me then. I was hurt and actually missing my former husband, while at the same time, was determined to show him that somebody loves me. I was so blind and broken I didn't take the time to properly evaluate who I was allowing to love me. He was my "yes" man. Yes to my every request. He didn't have a no in him. While I struggled with missing my ex-husband, I was on my way down the aisle again. My addiction was in full-fledge. Not to mention, the church was the fuel behind this one. Man, I couldn't even think straight because of the guilt associated with the pressure to marry because I was an active church member. I think this marriage could've been prevented had I been encouraged to date properly as a woman who was serving in ministry instead of marrying him because it makes the ministry look good. But marry I did. It was short-lived because one day I woke up and realized this is not it. This is a boy. Another marriage ended in divorce and we went our separate ways!

I began to talk to my Savior, Jesus Christ, about all of these failed relationships and marriages I was in. Wrapped in guilt and shame, I was sure I was done with marriage. I decided to get some help because I finally realized that there was an issue and it was within me. I was too open and didn't take time to analyze and really get to know a person. I was accepting before knowing all the facts or taking time to allow the facts to manifest. Not really taking the vows seriously. How could I? I certainly didn't seek the Lord about any of these marriages. So here I was - a woman who had been married multiple times, recovering from physical abuse, psychological abuse, verbal abuse, and my addictions. My addiction to run from all of my problems and to marry. I was a wreck. During my countless therapy sessions, I was able to sort out a lot about myself. I was able to gain clarity about the importance of evaluating and setting boundaries while learning a person before committing to marry. It was tough but I was determined to overcome my addiction. I longed to be a wife. I began to pray and tell the Lord I desired to be a wife but I needed His help and guidance. I said, "Lord, help me to date and get to know the man and he likewise get to know me." I was broken inside and was in dire need of inward healing.

Then, when I least expected it, I met someone. My thoughts were to date him and actually get to know him. And I did just that. There was no rush to get down the aisle. I was actually fearful. The Bible says in Proverbs 18:22, "he that finds a wife finds a good thing and obtains favor from the Lord." This man asked me to marry him and for the first time, I was scared. I was shaking in my boots. I said yes, but I hesitated on the planning. I knew I overcame my addiction because we delayed setting a date to get married so we could get to know each other even better. I went back to therapy to help sort out all of these feelings I was experiencing. Thank God I was able to sort those feelings out and make a wise decision. Some time transpired, three years to be exact, and my now husband and I got married. I understand now that it takes hard work and dedication to sustain any type of relationship. I'm proud to say we have been married for seven years now. I'm so thankful to God for the peace He brings in the midst of my stormy seasons in life. I feel that addictions are there and you have to work constantly to keep them at bay. I believe with a strong support system and a higher power, you can overcome and conquer any challenges in your life. With Jesus being my Higher Power, I can do all things through Him because He strengthens me.

Karen Bailey Robinson, a North Carolina native, is a retired housewife by day and an aspiring actor by night. Sometime in between, she is the biological mother to a beautiful daughter (Kayla) and two sons (Bautista and Victor Jr.) and adoptive mother to her two nieces (Tameika and Malaysia). She is an ordained Elder in the Lord's church and she enjoys working for the Lord in any capacity for she is a servant leader at heart. Karen studied Human Service and Drug and Alcohol Counseling at Delaware Technical Community College in Wilmington, Delaware. In her spare time, she enjoys singing, acting, reading, and spending quality time with her grandchildren. Karen is a co-author of Amazon's Best-Seller, After the Storm, and she currently resides in Philadelphia sharing life with the love of her life, Khalif.

You can connect with her on Facebook: https://www.facebook.com/cherlydine.bailey

Does Grief Ever End?
Leona Smith

Does grief ever end? I always battled low self-esteem as a child due to being bullied in school. I did a lot of things by myself at a young age because I was the youngest sibling born into the family. My mother was 37 years old and my father was 50 years old at the time of my birth. My parents are now both deceased. They were great parents who did the best that they could do to raise me. My mother had been blind since the age of sixteen. She also had a lot of medical issues such as high blood pressure and diabetes that developed while she was pregnant with me. Ultimately, these health issues caused her to suffer from chronic kidney failure overtime. She departed this life on August 3, 2020. My father also developed diabetes and high blood pressure. He ultimately died of what I believe to be a heartache! He departed this life on March 19, 2014.

Leona Smith

I took on a role of a caretaker and advocate at a very young age. I never needed or wanted for anything as a child, but I did grow up lonely and isolated - again, because my elder siblings were already grown with children by the time I was born. I was taught by my mom to apply myself in school. I believed in praying every night before bed and before every test to get me through school. I was a little girl who loved my parents' company, church, and my food. I began to gain weight around the age of eight years old which led to kids teasing me every day. Bullying really had a big effect on me. I remember getting off the bus crying to my mom every day because of being so overwhelmed from the day. My mom would always tell me that I didn't need those friends because I had her. I would indulge in food for comfort. I wanted big portions of food. I wanted all of my food to be extra. I didn't want one of anything! I have learned overtime that overeating for me was a sign of the disease of addiction surfacing at a young age. I used food to cope with all of my emotions until I became a teenager. Then, I started trying to fill the void I had inside with relationships. The peer pressure as a young adult and the need I had to feel accepted caused me to be a people pleaser! I would do anything to keep my friends or boyfriends happy.

I left home at age 17 and started being rebellious against my parents. I began hanging with friends who were smoking weed and popping pills that my mother tried to warn me about. These friends knew my parents were prescribed the medication that they liked to take. Ultimately, I began to steal the pill bottles out of my parents' medicine cabinet to give to them and to take myself. I would skip school in my senior year after partying all weekend. I surprisingly graduated high school in 2013 after missing a lot of classes. I felt like I had a need to be controlled. I would let other people tell me what I was going to do, where I was going to go, and who I was going to be around. I had a chronic desire to be available for people who were so undeserving of my care and my time. These friends/associates had only one desire and that was to get what they could get from me. I have learned now that a lot of people who were around me then weren't there for me, but were around me for what I had to offer - which was a ride, a good time, and a way to get high! I was addicted to a dangerous lifestyle. I felt like the more I did for people, it would be a way to be accepted. I even carried this mindset into adulthood which led to abusive relationships with guys.

Although I was living life on the edge, I still enrolled in community college for nursing. I would go to my classes but I needed my pills to give me the energy and I felt like they helped me focus better. When I was 18, my dad passed away and my life really took a turn. I eventually dropped out of college and became pregnant with my oldest son shortly after he died. I was trying to figure out how to deal with life without my dad by my side and how to be a mom. I was not only dealing with the grief of losing my dad but I was traumatized by the way I lost my dad. He died suddenly from a heart attack and I had tried to save his life by giving him CPR while he was lying on the floor. I remember looking into his eyes as he took his last few breaths. He was a true fighter! I knew I had to stay strong to help with my mom and to have a healthy pregnancy. I delivered a healthy baby boy on February 3, 2015, but I still couldn't deal with the pain of losing my dad. My oldest son was crawling around by the time I decided to pick up a habit of sniffing cocaine. I remember just wanting to feel numb so that I wouldn't have to relive the horrific scene of my dad's last moments. I still worked a job as a functional addict for several years before the disease needed to be fed more and more.

The disease of addiction is cunning and baffling. I gave birth to my second son on January 18, 2018 and I began to smoke crack cocaine after he was born. My life really started to spiral downward after this. I felt like I had lost all morals and I really didn't know or understand how I had even ended up where I was. I would steal what I wanted. I would lie to get what I needed to get and I ended up in jail several times for missing court dates and other petty, irresponsible reasons. I was literally running for my life. I walked the streets every day looking for just one more hit. The lifestyle I was living eventually caught up with me as DSS got involved. I had two children at the time that I was not taking care of the way I should. I remember feeling like I had absolutely given up on everything I had ever been taught in life. You would think I would have stopped using drugs right after DSS got involved, but I didn't! I walked around in despair with a fake smile on my face all while hurting deeply inside. I was facing losing custody of my children and I just couldn't stop using drugs no matter how much I tried.

My mother tried all she could to get my attention. I remember her saying to me that she had people praying for me. People were telling me that I shouldn't be doing drugs and I needed to get home to my babies. I do believe God sent ministering angels to meet me right where I was. Every night I cried myself to sleep begging and pleading to God to help me. I tried several attempts to stop doing drugs but I could not. I was doing the same thing expecting different results. One day, I just had enough of living the same way. I drove down the road to a church where my son attended. I remember feeling content the whole service until the end. Something indescribable came over me and I stood up. Before I knew it, I had fallen to the floor under such power. I have since learned that power was the power from NOBODY BUT GOD! The Holy Ghost fell upon me on that day of October 21, 2018. I left church that Sunday a changed woman. I was living with a dope dealer in the house where I laid my head every night and I got up clean and sober every day since then because Jesus took the taste away for any mind or mood-altering substance immediately! I got my kids back the same week all of this took place. I accepted an opportunity that came open at a transitional housing rehab with my children to learn how to become a mother and a productive member of society. I also gained that structure that I didn't have as a child. I learned to give my kids and myself a routine every day. I learned how to let go of that guilt

Does Grief Ever End?

I carried for so long thinking I could have done something differently to save my dad. In reality, I surrendered and accepted that God is the only one who gives life and He is the only one who can take it. I let God's business be His business alone. I have learned I don't have bad days; I just have learning days.

Since my transformation, I have given birth to two more handsome sons - one on June 19, 2019 and another on February 16, 2021. Today, I take every day one day at a time with the help of the good Lord. I am not perfect and everyday isn't always easy, but I know it's worth it. I just have to ask God for guidance in my daily walk, no matter the circumstances. I attend an awesome church, Grace Church, under great leadership and I'm thankful for the fellowship and support of my church family. Even when I fall or I'm just dealing with life, I know that in the midst of it all, God's got me. I serve a good, merciful God that I know will see me through. Grief doesn't end, but I find healthy ways to get through the pain and God's presence sustains it all.

As I continue on my journey, I'm grateful to have my wonderful husband who I married in

2021 by my side. My hope is to start a non-profit organization in the future that helps young ladies and men who are suffering from the disease of addiction and/or homelessness. I strive to be the best that I can be no matter what that looks like as long as I know that I tried my best to make the right decision. I want my kids to know that mommy fought for them, but more importantly, for herself. I hope that the demonstration of God's power working in my life encourages someone else that what He did for me, He can also do for you!

Leona Smith was born on July 19, 1995 to Isaiah Chancy, Jr. and Patricia Smith as the youngest of four children. Raised in Rowland, NC, she is a graduate of Purnell Swett High School. As someone who has a lived experience of substance abuse and mental health issues, Leona works as a Peer Support Specialist to encourage and guide individuals who are still struggling on their journey to recovery. Moreover, she volunteers as a Recovery Ambassador for the community through Stop the Pain, a non-profit organization. Leona is also a devoted ambassador for Jesus and is happily married with four children who she loves dearly. In her free time, she enjoys visits to the beach with her family, thrift shopping and pampering herself.

Acknowledgements

Thomas & Natalie Scott
Grace Church
Facebook: Grace Church, Rowland, NC
Instagram: @_grace.church

Elizabeth Blue

Summer Bullard

Rosa Locklear

Mi Vida Loca - My Crazy Life
Lisa Rodriguez Spaulding

My crazy life began when I was four years old. My mom and dad divorced. I felt as if my father had divorced me too because he left and never looked back. I thought I didn't know him at all because all I knew is what my mom told me and that was that he was an abuser and a cheater. Because of this, I never felt like I was missing out on anything from him. But I was a little girl who didn't understand. Then, while lacking a father, when I was five years old, the only other father figure in my life began molesting me. Yes, I was just a little girl who was being molested by her grandfather, my mother's dad. I remember him telling me, "It don't matter who you tell; they are not going to do anything to me." Boy was he right.

Going back to the day in Freeport, TX where we lived, my grandmother was driving and my mom was in the passenger seat. I was in the back seat in the middle. Remember in the 80's when seatbelts weren't really used and we all loved sitting in the middle so we could see outside through the windshield too? We were at a stop sign when I felt safe enough to say something, so I did. I said, "Papi has been touching me in my private areas and has been making me touch him back." My mom and grandmother both turned and looked at me and my mom started crying, saying he had done the same thing to her when she was little. My mom was maybe 21 years old when I was five. Aside from that one line that my mom said, they were quiet the rest of the drive. I don't even remember anything being said to my grandfather. What I do remember is him always ridiculing me and saying, "I told you nothing was going to be done," as he would laugh.

I had no idea that me speaking up would lead to my life turning upside down. My uncle, my mom's brother, came to take me to the beach with his family one day. All he wanted to do was ask me why I was saying those things. I was so hurt and was crying out. I was a little girl. Why didn't anyone protect me? As time passed, we moved to Houston and there came my grandfather laughing and still making fun about no one doing anything to him. And he was right. No one did anything. I was alone.

Years passed and I started getting bigger. I think I was eight years old when I got into my first fist fight. At that point, I was not going to let anyone hurt me again. I was angry. I was hurt. I was molested and I had feelings that no little girl should have at that young age. At this point, my mom couldn't deal with how bad I was so she sent me to live with my uncle and his wife and kids in Angleton, TX. I remember how much I prayed and begged God to let me go home but my mom never came for me. My aunt was good to me though. She would help me with my homework and always cooked for us, something I was not used to at home. When my uncle would take me to see my mom, I remember running from him and hiding so he would leave me there, but they always found me and I had to go back. My mom didn't get me until they were moving to the Rio Grande Valley. This was roughly a year later and I changed schools again for probably the tenth time at this point. Of course, every new school I went to I had to prove myself. Fighting to defend myself was the only thing I knew how to do. I got kicked out of so many different schools that eventually the administration wanted me out of their school district. My reputation was that I was a fighter and supposedly called a gang leader because people would follow me. Elementary and Junior High were probably the worst, but I didn't care. I was going to let everyone know that I was not scared of them. Always being the new kid was hard so I had to fight my way out of every situation.

A few years in the Valley and this man (my grandfather) was still around, but by this time he knew I would fight him and everyone that came at me. Man, woman, I didn't care. They moved back to Freeport when I was 15 years old. I was sexually active and was looking for love in all the wrong places. But really, at 15 what did I know about love? I know I had that craving that I needed satisfied though. I was with older men and at 16, I became pregnant by a 24-year-old man. How could this happen? Why wasn't anyone telling me no? Where was the adult supervision? Where was the person who should've shown me how to be a lady? How to take care of myself? All these things I had to learn on my own. My mother was too busy living her life that she did not worry about me. Remember, she allowed this man to be around me after she had suffered the same sexual molestation years before. So why did she allow her daughter to be around this predator?

At 17, I had my first son and I knew I needed to change because I was a mother now and I could've been anything - from a prostitute, alcoholic, drug addict, anything, but I chose to be a mother. I was going to love and raise my child differently. He would not suffer like I did. So I stopped going to school and got my GED. I started working to take care of my child, but then at 18, I had another baby - two babies at such a young age. I couldn't control that sex craving. I needed it. But now what was I supposed to do? I knew what I had to do. By the time I was 23, I had four kids and the only thing I knew was that this horrible cycle would be broken with my kids. I made sure they went to the same schools their whole life. I made sure they had everything they needed. I made sure to teach my daughter how to be a lady. I talked about everything with my children - from sex, to drugs, everything. They were my best friends. My life was complete because I had four kids who loved me so much and I adored them. I would never allow them to go around that man without me being right there.

Finally, when my children were old enough, I told them the story. My oldest son was so upset. He said, "Mom, I'm gonna hurt him." I said, "no son, let God handle that baby." I said this then and I say it now, my children are what saved me from being anything other than a great mother. My abuse led to me being sexually active at a young age, overly active even, but my children were the light at the end of this very dark tunnel. I still ask God why my mom allowed the abuse to happen to me. I know she was a young mom too, but still…I guess I will never have that question answered. It's okay now. I left it all in God's hands because it was too much for me to handle on my own. So to the young ladies out there who are going or have been in a similar situation, please find an adult you can trust. Talk to someone. Please don't go through this alone. Seek help so that you can heal and not allow yourself to get caught up in unhealthy habits like craving sex with men who don't mean you any good. Take back your power so that you can make wise decisions. You can always reach out to me too at lisaspaulding@ymail.com. I will always be here to help as much as I can.

Lisa Rodriguez Spaulding

Lisa Rodriguez Spaulding was born and raised in Texas and is a mother of four. In 2016, her oldest son was murdered at just 22 years old. Since then, Lisa has cherished her time with her family even more, spending quality time with those she loves as much as she can. When she is not at work, she loves going to the beach listening to the waves as they bring her peace and spoiling her grandbabies.

Conclusion

Congratulations! You made it to the end of this book. Hopefully, if you are on a journey to recovery, you found some inspiration to be consistent to the finish line. Know that you are not alone. There are resources to assist you successfully regain your sense of self. As the authors mentioned, it's best to find what works for you. That could be having a level of self-discipline to overturn your addiction on your own. It could be praying and going to church where you are supported. Assistance could also look like seeking the professional guidance of a counselor or other professional resources. Whatever you decide, do not be ashamed. Focus on your healing so that you can live the full life that God intended for you.

www.ingramcontent.com/pod-product-compliance
Lightning Source LLC
Chambersburg PA
CBHW070107100426
42743CB00012B/2671